HOUSE OF MOON

HOUSE OF MOON

DAVID HARTNETT

Secker & Warburg
POETRY

First published in Great Britain 1988 by
Martin Secker & Warburg Limited
Michelin House, 81 Fulham Road,
London SW3 6RB

British Library Cataloguing in Publication Data

Hartnett, David
    House of moon.
    I. Title
    821'.914

ISBN 0-436-19151-2

Printed and bound in Great Britain by
Biddles Ltd, Guildford and King's Lynn

TO MARGARET, EDWARD AND SARAH

CONTENTS

ACKNOWLEDGEMENTS

Acknowledgements are due to the following:

Firebird 4 (Penguin Books), *Poetry Canada Review*, *Poetry Durham*, *Poetry Now*, *Poetry Review*, *The Rialto*, *Sunday Times*, *Times Literary Supplement*

A number of poems have been broadcast by BBC Radio 3.

An earlier version of 'Seven Songs from a Halfway House' was first published in *A Signalled Love* (Anvil).

'House of Moon' won a prize in the 1985 *TLS*/Cheltenham Festival Poetry Competition.

DARKNESSES

Just now when I stepped downstairs from putting my son to bed
The back door blew open. Turning to shut it I gazed
Up across Joles Bank (wind-terraced, churned) and saw
On the summit this dim seed-husk dusting the darkness.

Your living-room lamp, father. Tonight perhaps you sit
Fronded by its glow, reading or looking up
Not at me but at this light squeezed behind from a darkness
He stirs in overhead, tired bird, our ruffled feather . . .

Father, there was a landing once, a child who listened
For echoed warmth – your cough, a crackled paper – webbing
Cocoons of light below; one night he flew in the darkness
Out of bed downstairs, aswoop on winged air . . .

Gone. And the wind flares. Suddenly like a sac
Your light is punctured, spilling rain. I close the door.
Behind me the stairs tilt and now almost as if
For the first time I am climbing them in the darkness.

WALKING MY SON TO SLEEP

Your breath, my breath, the wind's . . .
Tonight our whole house
Rocks in the wind's arms:
You won't remember this.

A breath, a pace, a breath:
We pass your cot once more –
The light on the landing splays
Yellowing spokes through the door.

Once, in a different house,
Next to another cot,
My breath came fast as yours:
I can't remember that.

A pace, a breath, a pace . . .
Rocking us together
This wind can't separate
Son from father.

Into a rim of dark
Each spoke disappears;
The cot they sliver past
Was empty for years.

I lay you in it now
As the night ends –
And dawn's mouth disperses
Your breath, my breath, the wind's . . .

MIRRORWORLD

'Who's that in there?' I whisper, drawing close
To the silver cave of drowned shadows
While, thinking to touch, you strain towards your twin
Out of my arms, blind to the ice between.

I carry you from the room then. Emptily
The glass glimmers still, becoming sky
Where, streaked with saliva mist, beyond eclipse,
Five tiny moon-discs glow: each whorled, a fingertip's . . .

FLOATING WORLD

July rain at the glass, its firefly prickles –
Squatted by a watering can, sucking a trowel
You tilt your face, half-listening, a half-
        Solemn one-year-old.

This is our bathysphere on a reef of summer:
Already beyond its belljar peace poplars
Swirl to the faint breathing of autumn currents
        Anemone tresses.

I hoist you up and you reach for the oleander.
When did its flushed star-clusters tremble and burst?
When will they set? Under this silver ceiling
        All seasons blur.

Under your dungarees I feel your heart,
A coral smoothness, pulsing, pored . . . You lift
Your fist and it is a frail-shelled nautilus
        Filtering light.

But the rain has slackened now. Minute by minute
Our cave unripples, clears. Beyond, like an ark
Moored to crumbling cliff-faces of cloud,
        The house uprears.

Pink meteors shower from the oleander's heart
When you twist to be put down. Hushed at the door,
Two surfaced divers, we pause – each breath a wave
        Chilling, then warm.

CHESTNUTS

Last night the sky for hours was sea was sky . . .
Now among herringbone leaves on the wracked lawn
They cluster, tide-motes in the wind's eye:
        Green echinoids.

You wander there, foreknowing through your smile
A day when the nubbed plates must split, a day
When cheese-pith pouches, tearing, shall reveal
        Tektitic hearts:

Dark twenty-year light still voyaging towards us –
And still through its leaf-veined shadow, climbing, climbing,
A boy looks down at the conkers on the grass
        Piled into cairns.

What was his hunt round autumn's frontiers for?
Under the sticky-buds games shattered some,
By spring the rest lay withered in a drawer
        And the tree could blossom.

Soon, your pockets crammed, you too will hoard
What today lies cast aside, a spendthrift wonder.
Above, the starfish reefs seem half prepared
        They tremble so.

I watch as from palm to palm this chestnut rolls.
You hand me its flattened twin and then, as if
Our touching fingertips exchange two jewels,
        Chalcedony flares.

TWO WINTERS

I was watching as my father shovelled snow
Outside the house we lived in years ago
And, mourning the furrowed white, had started calling
Stop through the glass when he vanished. Snow was still falling

As we went, my son (this palm a small hand's sheath),
On your first winter walk. Our mouths smoked breath
And coiled it in wreaths for a statue of boy Pan
Peeping from his cloak of flakes, his caked pipes frozen.

A boy (I said) *once dreamed snow fell for years*
Till houses and gardens were gone and the rays of stars
Like birds' feet flecked the white . . . then stroked stone curls:
You had slipped my grasp. Your firm prints faded miles.

Then, as the teeming air milled on the land,
I felt a shovel's weight ghosting my hand –
From the house my father was mouthing as if to shout,
The shovel grew feathersoft, hollow as a flute.

THE DANDELION CLOCK

Thunder all afternoon was a door in the silence.
Now we had walked outside under the chestnuts
Where dandelions seed. You crouched down – one breath
And a thousand wandering lamps had flared and melted
The air away. I laughed and said aloud
(To one who can barely talk) 'What time is it?'

Time to come in she calls from a flushed doorway
Jewelling chestnut leaves – *In from the storm.*
But he has just breathed on a plucked dandelion
And, smeared with bitter milks, must watch the seeds
Float among cones of flying ants spiring
Home to a lightning fault. *Not time* he says.

How long did I stay in the garden that afternoon?
Did my mother call again? When did the doorway
Clench its rusted petals? Soon the thunder
Would have seeded in dark rooms, the lightning washed
Windows of a thousand lamps, a thousand profiles;
Soon I would have dreamed of the dandelion's spineless echinoid.

The storm was about to break. Uncrouching you held
Up another wisped globe with a smile that said
'Again, again' as if somehow by breathing
I should tell the time. 'Time to go in' I said
As the first wandering raindrop fell and smeared
Your cheek like a tear, someone else's tear.

BOY ON A SWING

Lost in its weightless arc, taking the strain –
A pendulum between the earth and sky –
His body drifts from my hands then back again.

Flaring through distances, a jet plane
Segments the blue with milky vertebrae
Lost in their weightless arc, taking the strain.

It is the simplest physics to explain
How legs make motion, folding at the knee –
His body drifts from my hands then back again.

Years ago in an orchard by a lane
Like him I shouted *Daddy, don't push, let me!*
Lost in my weightless arc, taking the strain.

Now those joyful words pivot on a pain:
Weighted with fatherhood, I have learnt why
His body drifts from my hands then back again.

The vapour trail has smeared to one grey chain.
Night swings near; the frame creaks sleepily:
Lost in its weightless arc, taking the strain,
His body drifts from my hands then back again.

THAT CIRCLING STREAM

'We could go on forever' I said aloud,
Half-unaware what toothed vaults were splaying
Black lantern-loaded ribs over my head,
Until the wood's sun-chilly chancel had
Ambered a mother and child's fluttery playing.

Was it *these* brambles we cleared just three years past?
You were still pregnant then and could not have guessed
How soon their recrudescence would rouse our seeking
For drupelets to spawn red suns from a winter's racking –
Some stems were thick by now as a baby's wrist.

And was it last night over wine in the dining room
When the zodiac vaulted our talk of children's birth-signs
And we swam a second time down that circling stream
(*Scorpio makes a Leo . . .*) until black panes
Skimmed our eyes with the faintest star-berry gleam?

My plastic bag oozy and weighted down,
I paused where the wood ends, stooping to drop
A constellated softness in your lap;
Gnomon-still, chin upon chest, our son
Stared at a shadow stretched along the grass: his own.

TO MY DAUGHTER, TEETHING

The earth has teeth –
Torridonian stump,
Canine of Dolomite –
And all, once, buried.

Tonight, one of her latest guests,
You relive those eras:
Sleep is a restless magma,
Cries fold your face.

And yet, however archaean,
This drama draws you to us:
Tomorrow a new peak's tip
May fleck your smile.

THE HAIRWASH

I

Now that the trees'
Chill furnaces
Are stoked and fanned
By September wind
And, spark after spark,
Up into the black,
The Ram, the Water Bearer, Perseus, rise –
Stand in this bath and tilt
Toward me your head's own tiny galaxies
Whose stars of soap
Froth along the blond
Andromeda spirals
Your hair unfurls,
Until, warm water pouring from my cup,
They stream and melt.

Although you cannot help but scream
When the water swirls
In eye or ear,
Once it was the air
So chill, so dry
That made you cry
And the labour-ward lights' alien dream:
That other September night
When for your skull's
Soft armature
– Still sleaked, birth-wet –
I shaped my hands in a cup
Then touched one trembling fingertip
To the fontanelle's
Star-steady pulse.

Once like you I cried
Hunched above a tin bath
My grandmother's jug had filled
By a range, in Birmingham, at night –
And again, as my grandfather towelled
My head dry I cried
Because his hand was too rough
Or the towel too hot
Or because on the scullery wall
Eolithic, magnified,
Our shadows had begun to struggle
As if in a life after death
And then I cried for the waters of darkness to subside
From the city, wave by wave –
Or for the stars to come out.

Giants in death
The ancestors are not warm,
They have gone to bathe
In the receding star-stream –
Small and warm and dry
Let your head lie
Now in this cave-cot,
And when your blankets net
Darkness with blue fire
Dream of that zodiac
Where man and woman, towel and soap
Wheel in their stellar sleep
Until, from a curtain's crack,
Unloosed, the sun's hair
Streams back.

A VENETIAN GLASS

'From the altar of dark ocean . . .' (Shelley)

I

Outside through the cries of other people's children,
Under the Adriatic's silken drift,
The summer I came here last is taking root –
Deep as Lido sand, shallow as sea-thrift.

But inside a shutter has folded away daylight
And there is nothing beyond this morning's tide
When, dome by dome, in the motor launch's wake,
The city sank down avenues of pile-and-cloud.

So I have turned now to this vase of lilies,
Knowing how soon each sheathed coral throat
Will petal the water's edge like gifts for a sea-god,
Though cast by one careless if they sink or float.

On every terrace
Hibiscus flowers:
Saffron ovens
For glass hours.

I have bought you these beads
Congealed from fire
In this city married
To the sea each year.

An old man seared them,
A youth plucked them out –
Their necks were looped
With drupelets of sweat.

(The years like that furnace
Simmer then cool:
When I came here first
We were strangers still.)

Now at your throat
Each coral sphere
Is a drowned lantern
Or mermaid's tear

(Through a hundred rooms
Dead beauties turn
White masks to the light
So their jewelleries burn;

And round the Lido
A watery hand
Scatters flecked beads
Of foam on the sand) –

Fifteen years,
Twelve of them ours:
Wear them for the time
Hibiscus flowers.

3

We stood peering in at the roped-off room.
Green silk rippled down the walls and under glass
Saurian vertebrae glinted: a dinner service,
Their family long extinct. Smiling you said
'There's no one now to care if we took them home.'

Home: the freckled mercury of a mirror?
The window's scorched white flue? Or, in between,
That space where we met with our own negatives
Masked in a century's dark, the spark of a moment?
Under their ripples the walls were all bone.

We took each other's photos by the window
Then leaning looked down into the courtyard:
Wisteria sea-snakes were coiling the green air
And, as if no one had seen them, marble steps
Folded to vaults black wavelets rippled through.

Querini Stampalia

Paddle in these glass silks, these shallows, child –
Already more than a child since we brought you here;
Paddle with your back to us and to this seashore
Where couples are driven like foam apart, together.

One evening I paused by the palms on the hotel terrace
Looking for the room where you slept. But a hundred shutters
Had folded down their eyelids and round the Lido
The drowned cables of waves unravelled, sighing.

Child, beyond those waves in a city of shrines
Lobelias lift mauve foam-flecks under glass
Shallowing madonna and son. Down spongy walls
White masks of Neptune streak a coral stream.

One day, alone, you may go there. Paddle for now
As though you knew how, when tonight's full moon
Trawls the empty piazzas, nothing adrift
In her glimmering shoals can quite sink for ever.

THE DRESSING GOWN

The old silk dressing gown lay bundled
At the bottom of the last tea chest. Dragging it up
I felt each slithered fold ruck to elude
The long unfamiliar noose of fingers.

Its pattern was orange chrysanthemums splashed
On a blaze of green gashed black. Who might once
Have worn them or how they had wreathed to rest
In this new house seemed past my knowing till breezes

Stroked the window open and wavering
Away into light, a veil now, silk lifted
On the old bedroom, my undressed body, yours
Shy at the door, diaphanous, fierily sheathed.

But cloud and my aching arms crumpled the veil
Too soon to cloth. What shadows since that night
Had those dry pores filtered, becoming
Always less and less perfumed, less and less strange?

Through a thin wall between us I could hear
The leaf-sigh of your hands still unpacking . . .
How many years between us, each a chest
Disgorging darknesses, the gowns of the dark?

But the sun returned and holding it up for light
To pierce once more I watched your gown, almost
A body itself now, shimmering for what
Seemed a lifetime, just within reach of my arms.

SHORES OF SHADOW

Unseen, now seen, from room to room, a figure
Slides, kindling lights in its wake, one sail
Then another, suddenly stretched taut
Until the whole house honeycombs, aglow.

I only stepped out before dinner to look at the stars
While you stood in the kitchen chopping parsley;
Now, unmoored, this ghost galleon flickers
On the shore of shadow, sluiced blue and yellow.

Mistress of those lit decks, my phantom pilot,
Where will the voyage be tonight? Down milky reefs
A jet's invisible fins pulse green, unstringing
Bubbles of a heart-beat necklace; the tide runs slow

And when I look back there is only the house again
You in the kitchen, your lips parted. I nod,
Unsure still if it is me they summon
Or others gathered at my side on the shore of shadow.

PREHISTORIES

Nearer than darkness, farther than the dawn
Thunder has woken you, all-seeing, blind,
Inside my body, waiting to be born.

Skilled in their tentative braille, my fingers turn
To trace through skin the moulding of a hand
Nearer than darkness, farther than the dawn.

Knowledge of love has taught me how to mourn:
Seeking the vanished years I shall descend
Inside my body, waiting to be born.

From a far room, unearthly and forlorn,
My son cries out in sleep but sleep won't end
Nearer than darkness, farther than the dawn.

I dreamt my mother cradled a sheaf of corn
To her bare breasts. The sheaf tipped and it rained
Inside my body, waiting to be born.

Woken by lightning, dreaming of light's return
A moorhen flutters in flags that rim the pond:
Nearer than darkness, farther than the dawn
Inside my body you wait still to be born.

He calls. The dutch barn echoes a reply
As, through barley waves, the combine swims;
At harvest he will hear his sister cry.

Disturbed from sleep the spotted night-moths fly
Up from bales he rolls across or climbs
Calling: the dutch barn echoes a reply.

One voice lives on as all the others die:
'When windrows lace the field with silver streams
At harvest you will hear your sister cry.'

All through these cliffs, a straw geology,
His first three summers seep their golden seams:
Recall (the dutch barn echoes a reply).

Into the sunlight's vaultless granary
The combine's dust-veil shimmers while he dreams
At harvest I will hear my sister cry.

A roe-deer dolphins the receding sea
Whose era ends in seed-dunes, stubble flames.
·He calls. The dutch barn echoes a reply.
At harvest he must hear his sister cry.

3

Into dark's delta, rain and leaves my tide,
Unborn I navigate this ship of sleep
Where flesh is water, merging to divide.

A boy – my father – climbs the tree that died
But pale piscina fungi tempt him deep
Into dark's delta, rain and leaves their tide.

My mother stands on registry steps, a bride:
Clipping her hair, winged ants mate and weep
Our flesh is water, merging to divide.

My brother flies to the loft where bats glide
Round beams whose fruit of suckling young must heap
Into dark's delta, rain and leaves their tide.

And I, in whom no voice has laughed or cried?
Hung in a dreamless balance I barely keep,
My flesh is water, merging to divide.

Dawn. From their felted ark *All floods subside*
The cockerels cry as light begins to seep
Out of dark's delta, rain and leaves its tide
Since flesh was water, merging to divide.

4

That night your cry was mine inside birth's cave
And sheets grew glacial, I shook with dread
To think the body's ice-age melts in love.

Prehistories of pain no man will live
Passed in an hour and were deposited
That night your cry was mine inside birth's cave.

Antlering shadow, sheathed in mask and glove,
What lascaux shamans chanted round my bed
Ah, let this body's ice-age melt in love?

Summoned you came. But I could not believe
How, squeezed between those thighs, my seam ran, red,
That night your cry was mine inside birth's cave.

Since then, with ochre tears, my womb must grieve,
Streaking on hollow walls lost limbs and head,
Until the body's ice-age melt in love.

I dream of fire, of flints ringing a grave.
Then wake. Orion flares, the hunter, dead.
Your hunger-cry is mine outside birth's cave:
It stops. Our bodies' ice-age melts in love.

HISTORIES

Remembering perhaps that I *liked history*
You dug this up at one of the jumble sales
You haunted in those last years, sallying forth
From a house whose hilly terrace was always *beneath* you
Across a seaside town far from your birthplace:

Livy's 'Early History of Rome' –
Now, from the moment you gave it me, no more
Than a hand's frail papyrus fraying to an arm
Chained with tumuli of ganglia
Survives, half blurred in the book I hold.

Unread then and still I let the pages rustle
Randomly open. A small dust sprinkles me
As the old lives flicker past, the old names:
Tarquin, Appius, Caeso . . . such papery sounds
Kindling a warmth, familiar, whisperable.

HOUSE OF MOON

In the house of moon he is still eating breakfast
In vest and braces, bent above the steam
From his porridge's whorled andromeda of sugar –
And, for the child who laughs, stroking white bristles
I've never seen anything like it in all my puff.

In the house of moon she is still lighting the fire
Knelt at its pyre of wood and crumpled paper,
Her fingers splaying the flames like orange velvet –
And, for the child who gasps, fingering plaits
That flick her waist: *It doesn't hurt anymore.*

House of moon you begin where the landing ends
Or up in the attic or underneath the stairs –
Your doors are always open and never lead me
To the whispering blind man shrunk in his last ward
Or the crematorium drapes drawn on her coffin.

THE WANDERER

The plump coifed Sister ushered you through the front door
Still dressed in that last summer's silk two-piece, your chest
Swathed with necklaces, their horseshoe strata rippling
      Four brown belemnites splayed at your breastbone.

I had to stoop to kiss your cheek and at once it changed
To caked mud mosaiced in rifts beneath the ball
Of a veined brachiopod, hooded, greyly aflicker.
      Three times the meter whirred. And then you whispered:

I slept well this afternoon. Smiling relief I noticed
My child trying to crawl at your feet: *Your greatgrandson.*
But you were growing taller and before I could lift him up
      Two cylindered granite legs had pierced the ceiling

Which you reappeared between when the Sister sidled forward:
Thinner now, her body swaddled in clouts agape
On white smeared brown, she turbaned your head with a quilt
  then traced
      A circle round you once, pointing to the hall.

When I reached the door it was open, the dolphin knocker still
  slapping.
Beyond where moors unspooled their surf I could just glimpse
A moon-yellow wedge in the darkness, orbitless, dissolving,
      As all the lights behind me tripped out.

TWO ANCIENTS

When the wind turns inside out
From beneath my bed he creeps
Uncoiling an ammonite
Of blistered caps:
Ambush me again
Down by the garden gate
So I may lay my palm
Where the blood beat.

When the moon breaks in two
She floats from my mirror's clutch
Dangling gobstoppers
In their wrinkled pouch:
Swallow one whole again
With 'Nanny, I'm going to die'
So I may kneel to wipe
Your reddened eye.

When clouds root in the roof
A willow-ware image
Rifts my breakfast bowl
Laval with porridge:
Then, on the crater's bed
By a stream, beneath a hill,
Two ancients lie together
Blue and still.

A CASUALTY

Long-haired, he stumbled to my bed, torn combat jacket
Snowed by moonlight and, up bare arms, pout-purple
Welts of the needle's barrage, flame-kissings, craters.

Poor casualty I whispered but, cradling a wrist
Where the blood still fought, he made his palm flower,
A Swoppet knight for stamen, halberd ported.

Then, from his face, the drugged years retreated
And, a small boy again, outside the schoolgate,
Let's be friends he murmured; I held my hand out.

But memory's flare was arching ahead through darkness:
Wargames at my house; defeat; a gap in the ranks;
His bulging pocket . . . the soldier fell between us,

A silver tear. *Traitor.* Smiling, he vanished.
I woke to skirmishing snow, each flake's chill wound
Healed by the air it pierced then melted through.

SWIMMING TOWARDS AUTUMN

Into your trough of melted skylines
Limb by limb I slide without reflection:
A forked albino tuber tapering
Through shallows of tesserae, green pillow-lavas.

Cask for cloud-husks, raindrop cullender,
Mirror where the sun expunges his heat-spots,
Your shell is gashed with Roman numerals,
Depth-marks, millennia, Mithraic shelves . . .

Soon I have entered the last sargasso of summer
Spattered with capsized honeysuckle hulls
And, emptied of their crushed velvet cargoes,
Bobbing carapaces, dark as barges.

How long before winter empties you, waking
The hibernating echoes in your lias bones?
Already treadmilling these chill chambers
I hug a sarcophagus heart-beat, ripple of marble.

The waves fold away their togas. Sloughing off
Transparent scales thinner than blood or water,
I shiver now above this shrinking shadow:
Gondwanaland, an ocean on the moon.

THE SEVENTH FRUIT

Going to pick apples I remembered the orchard:
How, in a green, after-sunset sea,
Corals of spurs would flicker, countlessly shoaled;
A child, I never doubted the year's abundance

But scaling ancient reefs would wonder down
To mother or father in the dusk *How will we ever*
Eat all of these . . . ? then, perching, listen to the pulse
Hidden by my shirt swagged with its sweet burden.

The orchard was grubbed up years ago for building.
Now, Septembers later, both feet on the ground,
I have twisted this crop of six from a young James Grieve –
Behind me, sleeved in mist, my children glimmer.

No voice says *These should be keepers* and I need only
Press against my chest to sense, hidden
Amongst the hoard, a seventh fruit, its skin
Forever chill, its bitter flesh unripening.

IN THE LAUNDERETTE OF DREAM

Steam pastes every pane
In the launderette of dream –
But the chairs are empty.

The wool and cotton ghosts
Go kissing on the wet air,
Grey hands appear . . .

Ignore them if you dare
And the wailing of their ghost women
Help us help us fold this.

You too have a wash to do –
It spills now at your feet
From a knotted sheet.

But where have the soiled clothes gone?
And the stitched crimson flame
Of your name on every one?

Here is only shed skin,
Seed, the fossil of a tear,
This photo like the Turin Shroud . .

When the watery ammonite
Nests in its cave of pearl
What whiteness will these spin?

Watch from an empty chair
As the grey hands reappear
Scooping your load in –

While beakers tilt, sift
Down their flaky shower –
A machine has shuddered on.

Hours pass. You doze,
Wake once to hear your mother
Or is it her mother's mother?

In the launderette of dream
We wash nothing out,
Still the stains worsen.

Dawn. Inside the warm drum
Clinging, a drowsy bat,
There is this stranger's sock;

While outside through new snow
Naked, hugging themselves,
The dead go.

AFTER THE STORM

The storm flown past, a wound awaited you:
At dawn leaf-haemorrhaged lawns that seeped to stain
The very house-wall: it was the chestnut, fallen.
For days then the nervous surgery of chainsaws,
Spouts of arcing wood-froth, amputations

And, when the trunk was sliced, annulations
Circling the years you had lived or would yet live.
One night sucked by their whirlpool you swam through a room
Where a child and an old man sat, playing draughts
At a polished heartwood table. Outside, trees creaked.

Another night, passing indoors, you felt a finger
Skim glass furred with a thousand salt crystals
– Chill tears of the storm, unageing, unabraded –
In the space the chestnut's death had hollowed lay
A shoreline, dark and treeless, steeply shelving.

And so you lived for a time in that scorched haze,
Sap-acrid, violated, after the storm . . .
Until the last fire's charcoal tongues trembled
To lick their bubbling sugar and, turning, you felt
The chainsaw dangling at your side, a sleep-numb limb.

SEVEN SONGS FROM A
HALFWAY HOUSE

I

Every view melts to a window,
Every window to tissuings of light,
Every groove of every record I play ripples out
Across dark waters, contiguously slow.

Upstairs in the empty bedroom
Tilted on a stave of air,
A mobile chimes. Who did I hook it there for
Looking over the fields that first day we came?

Tell me we lived here once and have just returned.
Through a half-open door at the back
I glimpse your thigh, sun-flecked, propping a book;
Bleached pages whirr into the wind.

2

All day the fingers of the berberis splay apart
Scraping our wall, its '1966'
Gouged beside '1857' in the bricks.
Somewhere a door slams shut.

When did we come here to live?
On the ash, green earrings shimmer in the breeze –
Seed pods: you called them bunches of keys.
Locked daylight dilates in a leaf.

Evening enters, is a cloudy room. The screech
Of owls when I go to close the sash draws soft
Reply from our son in sleep. Faint wing-tips sift
The twilight, islanded, out of reach.

3

The pondwater thickens to mercury,
Every ripple when I look at it is slowed –
Nothing underneath but quiverings of cloud,
A clouded complicity.

Everything has long since occurred:
The ash buds unburnt to a polishing of coals,
The midday *kwiek* of the Little owls
Seeped from night's phial, unstoppered.

Where can we go now that is not elsewhere?
Already behind the locked front door
Sunlight pastes thin panes on our furniture
As though it were no longer there.

4

The laurel flakes stone shadows from the hod
I crouch by, hand on shovel. Down the field
Two solder tears of headlights roll, congealed;
Coal pushes its glittering flood

From the bunker's mouth, making you hear snow
Being scraped and swept (you'll say, when the fire is lit)
Around some girlhood house. Curled in a second's nugget
Flame-fossils glow.

This scree I scatter will lie hieroglyphed
Tonight with frost. I slam the trap down,
Ratcheting a pheasant from the laurel – each wing-flap blown
Back to me whirring: loud, soft.

5

Into my shaving mirror the road
Wavers, swaddled by veils of autumn rain;
The sky is a broken sliver from a pane
Stuffed with cardboard, corrugating cloud.

Someone else is waiting to move in:
The soft fly-pyramids rise and fall
Behind me. The ghost of a prayer-wheel
Moans inside a plastic fan:

His voice, who lived here before
And longs once again to stand
Like a branch warped beneath the skin of the pond
In the bricked-up window on the stair.

6

Cresting and troughing the motor mower drones
Folding waves in air, shaved emerald.
Who will ever remember how a child
Learned beside this hearth to crawl once,

Unless, across the empty bedroom floor,
They see a red-legged partridge feather drift . . . ?
No one you say came just now to lift
That latch on the front door.

At half-past five in the whorls of a dustbin's shell
The wind's bruised lamps ignite –
Days in the house are water tugged towards night
Wave upon wave, unfolding, parallel.

7

Invisible, a stream risen from somewhere
Underground, trickles between door and open door,
The house is vesselled with chill alveoles of air,
Sunscorched corpuscles askim there . . .

Cloud-aquariums brim each window-pane,
Oak trees, polyping the damp glass,
Effloresce into blue endlessness,
Every twig crumbling to root again.

There is nothing that is not circling, unstopped –
Yet one day, by that skirting-board,
Someone may brush, dust-ravelled, this brittle weed:
Filaments of our scissored hair, unswept.

WORDSONGS

1

The clouds are seeping snowlight; no snow has fallen.
In the snarled net of an oak the wind lunges;
Half my life I have stood here watching, waiting
For words, their chill essence, half-tasted, melting.

On the pond, under the oak, two Muscovies
Melt into the water, two white reflections;
White feathers fall to the water from arched wings –
The wind has ballooned free now, the snowlight faded.

2

Leaf-cave-heads, green sieves of air and rain,
Clustering to my window in the simmer
Of a thunder-nourished silence: summer by summer
I have waited for your masks to whisper again.

Take my mask today, mouthing at this pane
Air-and-aquarium nothings; open the cave
Where your heads toss together another year's leaves –
Toss my words a little in your sieves of rain.

CLIPPING THE PEACOCKS

One thunderous day I trapped them in an outhouse –
Thick and green, a feathered mirror of flight,
The air cracked as their wings cracked, swirling light –
From beak to beak fear clicked its rapid morse.

With a roll of netlon and my secateurs
I was the retiarius in that arena –
One by one I clamped them between my knees,
Sad gladiators cased in glimmery armour.

When blades sheared the arc of the first splayed wing
I sensed a thousand unseen threads snapping:
Oaks severed from ashes, twilights from dawns –
Under their plumes jet eyes mourned all distance.

I left them cowed but defiant there. Night came
And they were flying together through a dream
Wailing from the tree-tops, lit by lightning flashes
And as they neared I saw their human faces.

Why such laborious art, such cunning to ground us,
Who long for flight yourself? Clipped wings must grow.
Their painted masks grew mocking, imperious –
I saw earth shrink to a bubble miles below.

My quilled Eumenides, grim Ariels,
What roosts awaited us, what airy hells?
And when at last your giant wings furled in peace
Whose body, a moulted feather, spun on through space?

THE REMEMBERERS

They whisper *war*:
When Coventry *went up* and the Brum horizon
Was a southern Borealis of saffron fire –
That *midnight dawn.*

Or else the haystack
Somewhere in Hertfordshire, one sleep's distance
From the hush of doodlebugs and yet they woke
Seething ants.

Not history yet
These memories have a life eluding time
Now in this sunlit garden where we sit
Rehearsing them.

A child shouts
Unseen among azalea galaxies;
Across the air a yellow gossamer floats
Spooled by breezes.

Perhaps the past was
Always this far away, always this close;
On deckchairs frothing sheets of yesterday's news
The rememberers doze.

Let night fall:
Then let me, leaving, glimpse in the wing-mirror
Two streams of light converge on a black hole
Or unborn star.

BEQUESTS

for Michael and Posy O'Neill

On the evening of the first day of the Somme
My mother's uncle woke to see his brother
Standing in battle-kit at the head of the bed –
Masked by the moon he stroked a pierced breast-pocket.

Killed in action was how the story ended;
Later, over a hand of gin rummy,
My mother's mother relit the fires and fireworks
Frilling Wren's Nest hill with their taut auroras
That night the relief of Mafeking came through.

How long before such memories merge with mine?
Retelling them I feel like a child again
Close to sleep, waiting for a kiss goodnight:

Again stairs squeak as a storm's echo dislodges
Plaster, spiders; again, at my window, the moon
Whirls, an ammonite catherine-wheel burning
Back to its cinder socket, its heart of ice.

★

Topping an egg one Sunday my father told
How he was the first in the spring of '36
To hike the high nevada into Spain,
'Travels with a Donkey' nestling in his rucksack:
A border guard I met knew what was coming . . .

Two years and he was writing home from Persia:
'So hot you could cook an omelette on the pavement.'

Under the deserts, the snows of war, I lay;
Yet now my birth certificate looks as creased
As the postcards that franked his travels; yellowing
Like that Stevenson soaked in a Pyrénéan thaw.

On the edge of sleep these echoes will flicker still
When, above the duvet's bleached craters,
A caped shadow rises, its helmeted mask
Whispering *Desorden señor, desorden soon* –
Its fist unfolded on an egg, a small chill moon.

★

Years earlier he had watched the Great War ending
From a window above Piccadilly: a peace parade
With cheering crowds and looped vines of bunting;
The soldiers were so distant *they could have been lead.*

As distant, now, these words – echoed maybe,
From a 1918 *Times*; yet, sleeping on them,
I have felt his face at the glass merge with mine:

The Bay of Pigs, 1961 –
From a classroom window I stare into the street
Where paper shells of houses craze and shrivel . . .

Already the soldiers had gone and it was time for bed.
Unseen, in a shop doorway, a couple swayed
Together, making love: her hobble skirts
Hoisted as if for a paddle at Southend –
When suddenly the moon rose, silking her thigh,
The mask of his face drained white as a child's, sleeping.

★

When the Birmingham raids began my mother's father
Grubbed up laurel for a shelter. Through the blackout,
On fire duty, he thought his daughter snug:
The darkness . . . spiders . . . I ran back to my room.

Next year she married my father. One moonlit night
A near miss caved their bedroom ceiling in –
Sheltering under the bed they waited for dawn
More snug for their blanketing of cratered ice.

I too went down a shelter once, on a dare:
The echo of an older boy's *Snug for two*
Sent shadows scuttling back into urinous darkness.

Tonight these are the echoes I must rekindle,
Daring myself to stir bleached limbs, to touch . . .
Until at the top of the steps in the moon I see him
Gasmasked, swinging a shovel and a bucket of sand:
Put out that light he shouts *and go to sleep.*

★

Before the war to end wars my father's uncle
Hid a Sinn Fein gunrunner in the basement –
His cat would *take the meat from a dying man's mouth.*

My father still had his faith when he sat at the feet
Of Chesterton in a Soho Four Ale bar:
Smoke wreathed the Catholic millennium –
One war later his leather-bound copy of 'Poems'
Leaned in his son's bedroom bookcase, forgotten.

Less strange to me now that young man supping beer
Than the boy enacting 'The Battle of Lepanto'
Or walking to school with a black plastic machine-gun
Hidden in his duffel-coat (it was confiscated).

Still in the pulsing flare of the muzzle's foreskin
He dreams of scimitar'd Turks, masked by moonlight
Who will slice him into smoking chops unless
Don John peeps round his door, mouthing *Sleep tight.*

★

Lloyd George had promised them all 'Homes fit for heroes'
But down on Hendon Common one hero dug in:
Cycling to school I would pass him: trench songs
He sang or shrieked 'Look out, it's a Woolly Bear!'

In the next war my father too slept rough:
Because of the Blitz. One night we chose a haystack –
So many earwigs she almost longed for bombs.

He promised to take me camping once, on Dartmoor.
For days I wandered alone in a No Man's Land
Of sleaked gunmetal tor and heathery sump,
Then shivered beneath taut canvas sucked by winds
Homelessly echoing . . . we never went.

Tonight when my curtains sucked against the window
I felt his breath on my cheek; the moon flared
And, muffled as if by a mask, again I heard
We're here because we're here because we're here.

KILLING THE ANTS

I

Why, her grey hair plaited to the waist,
Does she lean beside the birdbath, kettle tilted,
Pouring an arc that flickers thundery air?
And why, his troops all fallen beside the pergola,
Does he crouch to see how, in her holocaust,
The winged ants on the path are shrivelled and melted?

And why, when she turns and slams the kitchen door,
Does thunder nest in his head and multiply
Becoming words, *her* words, heavy with war
As, gripping the loaf, she scoops up butter and smears?
It would be close as this – they were all volunteers,
Singing as they marched to the station (lightning-riven
Faces, white as larvae, falling from the sky . . .);
And why, when he wonders, *What is thunder for?*
As she tucks him up in bed, does a voice reply
The dead are marching to battle now in heaven?

And why do winged ants spiralling through his dream
Turn to tiny wounded men that teem
And flicker all night against the window-pane
Of a room where, twenty years later, she will lie
And he, whisper a grandson's words again:
I think, yes, I think, you will always be too old to die,
Only to hear thunder, the echo of a cry:
Why are we born to wars each century,
Each minute breathing the deaths of a thousand things?
Why that stormy day, did the soldiers start to sing?
Words that in the after-silence seem
Uncapturable as the marriage-flight of wings,
Transparent as the armies of the rain
That fall and flicker now, not knowing why.

What has he found behind the raspberry cage,
Talused against an elm bole? Is it a nest?
What does he hope to find inside the nest,
Poking his twig in, squirming it? Are they ants?
What is this skimming above the swarms of ants:
That toy Bristol Bomber his uncle gave him?
Are these the kinds of presents he wants to give them:
Bombs of dry earth, small stones and Ship matches?
Hasn't he heard it's dangerous to play with matches,
Shouting 'We're hit', kindling the wing's plastic?
Or doesn't he know that, once on fire, plastic
Will melt and rope, weeping a wet furnace?
Doesn't he care what bodies crisp in that furnace?
(Only last night his uncle mentioned Dresden.)
Does he imagine hovering above Dresden?
(*Dead reckoning we called it, flying blind.*)
Have the *thousand furnaces beneath us* struck him blind
So that he staggers back rubbing his eyes?
Or is it merely smoke stinging his eyes
Now he has ringed the nest with burning newspaper?
What are all the wars he scribbled once on white paper
To this warm darkness he squats by without words?
Soon there will be more darkness and his uncle's words
(*Firestorm. Apocalypse. A bomber's moon.*)
Will come with masked ants droning across the moon.
Must there always be this chamber in his head, hollow as a
    shell,
Where the dead with their words lie wadded, shell by shell?
When will my words coagulate on this page –
Pools of a burnt bomber badging the last scorched page
Among the ashes of a child's war waged
Years back behind the raspberry cage?

THE PILOT WHO CAME BACK

That afternoon it was the Battle of Britain
I refought on the floor of the chalk quarry:
Round and round, sleek fin on silver fin,
Airfix Spitfire and Focke-Wulf went twirling
Until the enemy plane stuttered then plunged
Down into screes of flint and honeycomb sponge-casts.
Out of sight on the slope above my father
Swung his irons; not long before my birth
He must have heard the engine-drone I mimicked
And seen this sky blossom a thousand explosions,
Years too deep or too high ever to scale now:
The blue-black skin of a pond wedged by wind,
Waterlilies unclenching chalky petals . . .

During a lull I sat amongst the scatter
And watched westering sunlight begin to pink
Strata that had all been water once . . .
Surely whatever had died here lived on still?
We heard the engine cut out and saw it spiral
Down into the quarry – one of theirs –
Never recovered – perhaps he sits there still.
(Stiff in the cockpit, bones laced with brambles,
A parachute's wet grey fungus clamped to his back . . .
Or else at the base of the cliff, stumbling from a cave
He had slept in those twenty years, his flying jacket
Aflash with zips, the teeth of cretaceous sharks,
And at his forehead, goggles, two compound eyes . . .)

A chill on the air made me call up to him,
Again
    Echoing
        He finds a foothold
Now, begins to scale the precipice

– Finned bird, legged fish – toward that void he fell from
– A twirling dandelion clock – forty years back . . .
All afternoon he climbs, all through my childhood.
I have never seen his face; nor has he gained
The summit yet – once, dislodged, a boulder
Plumes toward me, clotting drifts of air.
Night falls and *Are you still down there?* calls my father,
His club's swung meteor silver-arced with stars.

ACROSS THE TOLLBRIDGE

'*O Stunden in der Kindheit,*
da hinter den Figuren mehr als nur
Vergangnes war und vor uns nicht die Zukunft.'
(Rilke)

Lying with his eyes closed and face pressed down
Into the ribbed imitation leather
On the back seat of his father's Ford Zephyr
The game is to imagine where they are
Now on the road that leads along the coast
Under the Downs (on Thundersbarrow Hill
The Saxons believed Thor himself was buried)
From his grandparents' house in Brighton across the tollbridge
And on under more Downs (Cissbury Ring
Where – he will read one day in Curwen's 'Archaeology' –
A nameless warrior race built ramparts once
During some long forgotten war) and on
Until they reach home. But nothing in the sounds
He hears seems ever to tell him where they are:
Not the wind's shrill twitter through an open window
Nor the radio's shriller cry of *Wikey Wikey*
(As though from within an ancient burial mound)
Nor even his mother whispering to his father
About grandad's 'gluecoma' – *It's getting worse;*
Coming back from Bournemouth across the tollbridge
He almost drove the Rover into the river:
It's all gone dark Lil she said he said.
Nothing . . . and when he opens his eyes again
They are always too far forward or too far back
And he must shut them again, shut them again.

So then the game is to imagine there is nothing
On the other side of the darkness that means his eyelids –
No car, no parents, no street, no earth at all –
All noises and all voices buried within him:
The city simply vanished in under a second –
The blast literally evaporated people,
Leaving mysterious scorch-marks among the rubble.
Those who watched the glare from miles away
Lost their sight forever but 'Switch it off,
Nothing for me to see' grandad had muttered
Buried by darkness beyond the flickering screen.
Remembering he opens his eyes as the car passes
That half-demolished terrace by the gasworks:
Rubble, a blackened fireplace peering out
Through rooms of wind and air – nothing has vanished.

Or the game could be to imagine they are nearer
Home than he had imagined, halfway across
The tollbridge above the Adur's ribbed grey mudflats
Scooped by sluggish silver, his father saying
(As he flicks Havana ash from a tweed cuff)
An ancient river this, imagine the ages
It takes for hills to be ground down into floodplains.
('And every mountain and hill shall be made low'
Black, as if scorched, the words flock up and hover.)
Centuries or a second – grandad's Rover
Ghosting the screen of his eyelids, spiralling down
Toward a wet darkness, spiralling, changing
Into a cigar, a silver bomb that blossoms
Millions of jewelled eyes, glowing forever.

Once the game was to imagine time going backwards
As if the streetlamps you saw meeting behind you
Were to flare out instead, wider and wider,
Until there were no streets, no houses, no towns
And it was the time they lived up on the Downs,

Like pigs grandad had said *in one-roomed hovels*
No cars, nowhere to go but he was watching
A tall long-haired man walking towards him,
Through gates set in a revetted chalk rampart,
His unclenched palm (a coin? a flint? a jewel?)
Pulsing red, redder . . . and he was watching
A woman crouched by scorched hearthstones, weeping
Over a fur-swaddled body on the tamped chalk,
Till a voice in the wind that always blew up there
Muttered *Before the flood of Noah, before*
The Assyrian came down like a wolf on the fold . . .
And opening his eyes again he saw the streetlamps
Callipering darkness, as before . . .

Soon, sooner than he thinks, the game will be
To imagine time hasn't passed or isn't passing –
The year of the Bay of Pigs, grandfather
Hospitalised for the first time (*No room,*
Nowhere to go out in the Rover now) or else
(Diluvian darknesses, more distant now than childhood!)
The year of a school study nicknamed 'The Hovel',
Sunset on the blue-spined book, glowing, opening:
'. . . a winter evening round behind the gashouse';
Byron sunk forever in those silver swirls;
Or the year of grandfather's death when, day after day
Turning from chalked-up Downs and Adur floodplain,
The bald geography master muttered *Hartnett!*
Your hair would have graced an Assyrian, get it cut.

Glaucous melting to glue . . . an ancient river
Silted among ash-ramparts, glaucous rubble . . .
On Thundersbarrow and Cissbury all the dead awaking,
Their ribs of chalk aglow, irradiated . . .
Long-haired warriors sucked streaming backwards
Into a streetlamp's flickering topaz eye
As the car-radio echoes *I can see for miles.*

56

The game is not to imagine in the end . . .

This man who sits with his back pressed to the footings
Of the whitewashed Martello tower on the quay;
Who clasps his drawn-up knees and wears a bandage
Turbanned about his head, shielding both eyes . . .
Whose hair is long, weed-braided, whose suit is wet;
If it *is* a suit – this silvered carapace . . .
This man, if it *is* a man and not some shadow
Scorched on the darkness of eyelids, the eyes of darkness . . .
Ferryman or warrior or ancient king . . .
Not to imagine the bevelled jewels, the scooped flints
Set in the socketed soles of his bare feet,
Their fires ruffled by the first breathings of darkness
To red, to silver-blue, to topaz, pulsing . . .

For when there is no game at all – this dreamer
Of someone else's death vanishing –
As the car arrives at the tollgate, suddenly,
Spontaneously, joyously, instead of paying
His father accelerates across the tollbridge
Making him laugh until he wants to cry
To see the dwindling tollkeeper stagger back
Under a silver shower flocking upwards
Out of fists clenched in the sun's red eye
Before, briefly yet almost as if forever,
It spirals down to the now invisible river.

THE OTHER SIDE OF
THE MOUNTAIN

(Kitzbühel, 195–)

for my parents

I

The cellar steps, the cellar's cube of light –
Stacked boots, ranked skis (ribs without number), clothes . . .
Squeezing my shoulder (*We'll need a big shovel*)
He dips down into the wax- and earth-sweet pit.

Waiting above I scuff half-melted snow:
Shadowy continents soon to be reborn
In sketch pads brimming anthropomorphic bears
Locked until doomsday in their bloodless wars.

Sunset. Outside the hushed hotel lounge
Our snowman stands guard. Spread on my knees
The paper darkens with hollow, outlined bodies.
The snowman's shadow bruises the snow grey-blue.

2

France had melted from our Snow Sport Special. Jolted
Awake to the couchette's green benthonic glow,
I glimpsed a platform, steam-swirled, grey-blue.
Austria, someone whispered. *We've crossed the border.*

And so, wide-eyed and ignorant of Europe –
Her wars, this last exhausted peace – a child
Gazed as a man stooped down the line to tap
Each coupling. Under his boots the snow-ribs creaked.

He crouched beside our carriage. Briefly coned
White in the lantern's flare his face swam by
Out of a frame from Battle Picture Library –
The stubble-blue mask, grey ghost of pain or love.

3

Wide-open for the lens my milk-tooth gaze
Barely betrays fear of the giant phantom –
Half bear, half snowman – pawing my left shoulder;
His outline stains the mountain like a bruise.

Where has he shambled from: what cave or high
Hotel bedroom? Through a mouth that is no mouth
But the socket of darknesses gutturals seethe,
Swirling their smoke. I long for the shutter's click.

Centuries late, down the hotel steps, my father
Descended to pay for this. Headless, slow,
Scuffing away through the snow's plashed-gold craters,
The bear had melted to a man, more ghostly now . . .

4

At evening on the floor of the hotel bedroom
I wrestled against his bear-hug, sometimes winning
(Jarred loose, a milk-tooth plopped onto the carpet);
Outside, shawled in stars, the bell-tower, leaning . . .

Afterwards he might tell me Blitz stories:
Doodlebugs skimming the hushed expectant houses,
A midnight drive across snake-knots of hoses,
The shrubbery 'Anderson', its sweet earth reek . . .

Panting with victory I boasted I knew
Every word there was to know in the world.
Tell me what a mammal is. The chill flicker
Of the bells numbed my tongue. *Warm-blooded, a bear.*

5

At the start of the junior slalom competition
A register was borne up the nursery slopes
And, like a fluttering bird, splayed wide open.
You had to enter your name. My turn next.

'DAV . . .' appeared before I froze.
Jewelled shawls of snow went swirling in the breeze.
Eyes of children, instructors' eyes, ringed me:
Soldiers dreaming of battle, quickened for the hush . . .

Say your name aloud. Lost, lacking wings,
My voice dipped down into frozen orphanings
Of mountain shadow. Someone coughed. The sun
Clouded, bruising my still white page grey-blue.

6

Who do you think's down there? he said in the hush
Of our jammed cable-car, a water droplet
Poised for the jewelled knife-glitter fathoms below.
I looked: rock-bruises, pines, our frozen shadow.

(*No one knew it was happening at the time.*
Europe. Cathodic blizzards swirl and hold them,
Stiff as if frozen, stacked, white bodies . . . Steps
Lead down to a cellar . . . Switch off. *Before you were born.*)

A mammal? *Yes. Perhaps a bear asleep.*
Hibernating. The hollow cube jolted
Then, as laughter plashed and fear melted,
Swung with its far blue shadow to higher ground.

7

My troops freeze in battle on the hotel terrace –
Ally and enemy stained the same grey-blue.
Some are already lost in the jewelled waste.
The snowman melts, forgotten. Home tomorrow.

Already, across my sketch-pad, carriages
Are fleeing in reverse, abandoning Europe,
A landscape sliced by windows, trunkless trees
And people without heads, melting to exile.

This afternoon for a last time I will snowplough
Down dark pine-avenues behind my father –
Ahead, poised above mountains, the white flare:
A million bevelled mirrors, reflecting nothing.

8

The hotel's cave, the hotel's steps of shadow –
Grey-blue ranks in the cellar: each sleepless ghost
Exiled, waiting for the bombs to cease or waiting
For windowless carriages to jolt east.

But upwards, too, past frozen sentries
Of snowman and bear the steps might rise again,
A doorway bezel daylight's bruised jewel –
Beyond will lie the other side of the mountain.

When the snow has melted, father, meet me there,
By grey rock-clefts the blue gentians flood;
Together we may look across a world
Stained by sunlight, fleet with shadow-mapped cloud.